How the Piloses Evolved Skinny Noses

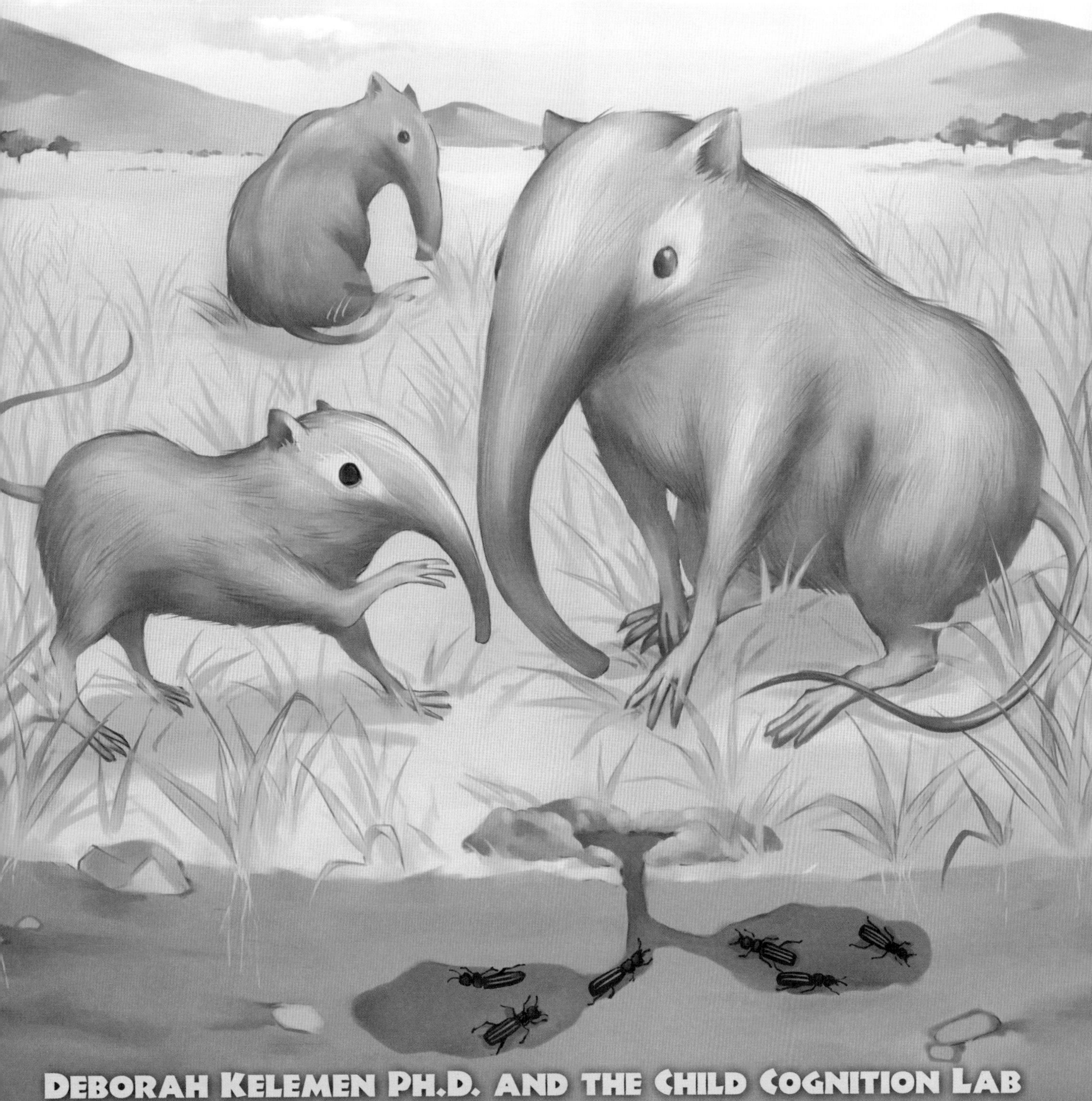

Deborah Kelemen Ph.D. and the Child Cognition Lab

How the Piloses Evolved Skinny Noses provides a simple explanation of biological adaptation. It is the first in a short series of picture storybooks aimed at introducing young children to the powerful, but widely misunderstood, concept of evolution by natural selection. Our overall goal is to help young learners understand this concept from an early age when they may find it easier to grasp, and to establish an early foundation for lifelong science literacy.

The natural process described in *How the Piloses Evolved Skinny Noses* is real. However, the piloses are a fictional species. Child development research indicates that children often find it easier to learn about animals when they do not have preconceived ideas about them.

More details on the research underlying the design and use of the book as well as supplementary teaching materials can be found on the Child Cognition Lab's Evolving Minds website at EvolvingMindsProject.org

For further information, contact:
Tumblehome Learning, Inc.
201 Newbury St, Suite 201
Boston, MA 02116
http://www.tumblehomelearning.com

Library of Congress Control Number:
2017937329

ISBN 978-1-943431-26-7

Kelemen, Ph.D., Deborah
How the Piloses Evolved Skinny Noses /
Deborah Kelemen, Ph.D. - 1st ed

Art: Chen-Hui Chang (張辰卉)

Printed in Taiwan
10 9 8 7 6 5 4 3 2 1

TUMBLEHOME learning

How The Piloses Evolved Skinny Noses

These animals are called piloses. This is how the group of fully-grown adult piloses looked a long time ago, many hundreds of years in the past. They were all piloses, but they looked a little bit different from each other. Many of the piloses had wider trunks, and only a small number had thinner trunks. Because these piloses lived many hundreds of years ago, and piloses only live to be about ten years old, each of these piloses are, of course, dead now.

Here are some different fully-grown adult piloses. These are the piloses that live nowadays, and this is what the group looks like now. Piloses nowadays mostly all have thinner trunks. Why were there so many piloses with wider trunks in the group a long time ago but nowadays there are mostly piloses with thinner trunks in the group? Why do piloses mostly have thinner trunks now? Let's read and find out!

Many hundreds of years ago, piloses wandered all over the meadow with their children. They had a busy life.

Because they were so busy, they felt hungry and thirsty a lot. They had to spend a lot of time looking for food to eat and water to drink.

The food that piloses ate were called milli bugs. The milli bugs moved about all over the meadow and under the ground.

When piloses ate these bugs their tummies felt full and they got healthy and strong. Healthy piloses lived for a long time and had enough energy to have many children.

But then the weather became very hot and sunny all of the time. And the ground went from being green and soft to being dry and hard. It's still very hot nowadays.

Because of the heat, the milli bugs went from moving about all over to moving about only underground where it was cool. Most of the bugs stayed at the very ends of thin underground tunnels.

The small number of piloses with thinner trunks could eat lots of milli bugs because their trunks could fit all the way to the bottom of the holes where most of the milli bugs lived.

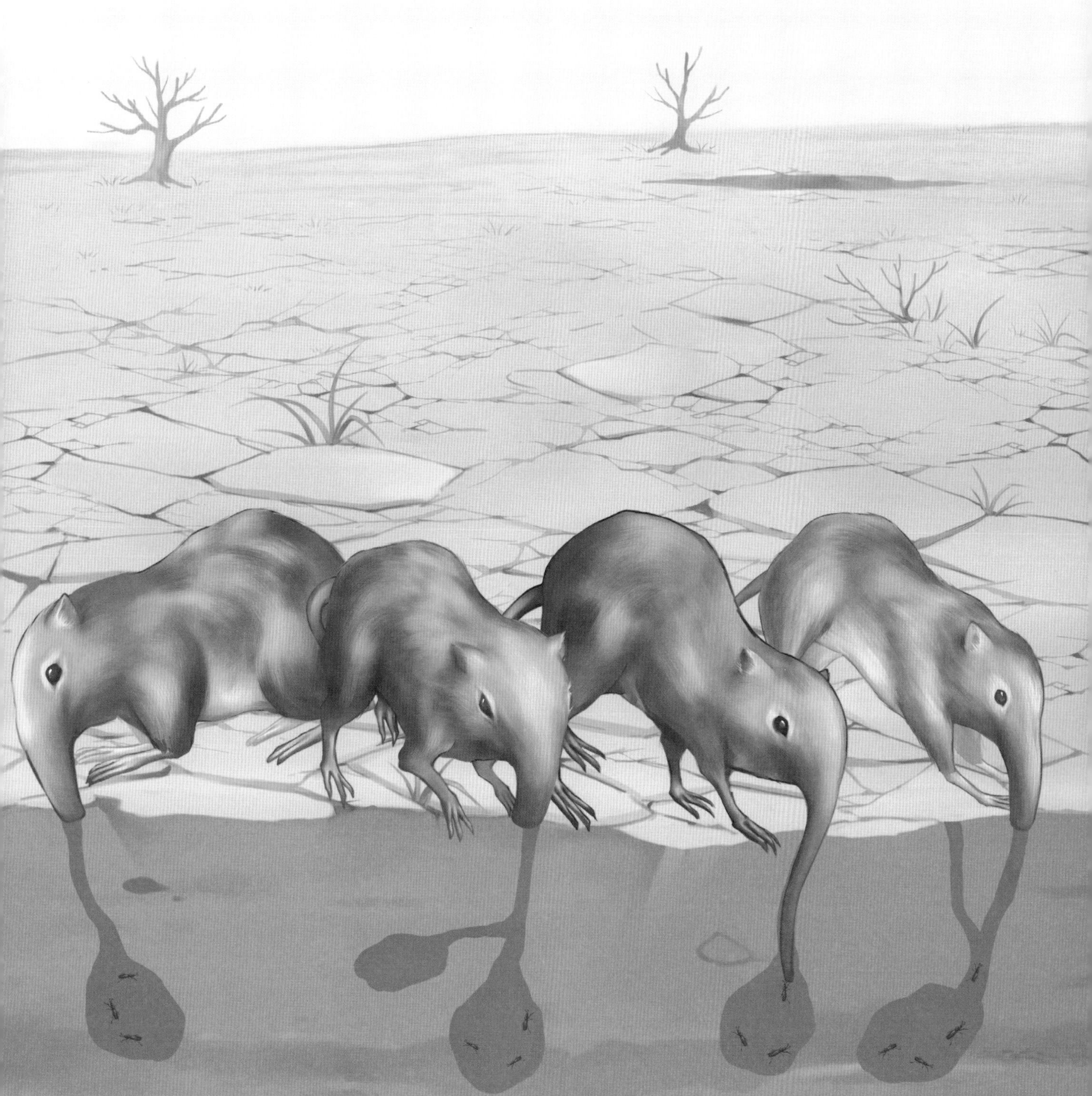

Piloses with wider trunks had trouble getting food. They could only fit the tips of their trunks into the holes. Some piloses with wider trunks got to eat when they found milli bugs that were moving about near the top. But other piloses with wider trunks did not eat anything at all.

The small number of piloses with thinner trunks were strong and healthy because of all the bugs they were eating.

Some piloses with wider trunks were able to reach a small number of bugs, so they were kind of healthy too. But other piloses with wider trunks couldn't get any food, so they became weaker and weaker and felt more and more tired. They did not have any energy at all.

The small number of piloses with thinner trunks were very healthy, so each of them lived for a long time and had enough energy to have many children. These children were born with thinner trunks because children were usually born with the same kind of trunk their parents were born with.

Some piloses with wider trunks were very weak. They were so unhealthy that they died before having any children. But other piloses with wider trunks were only healthy enough to have one child. And that child was born with a wider trunk because its parents were born with wider trunks.

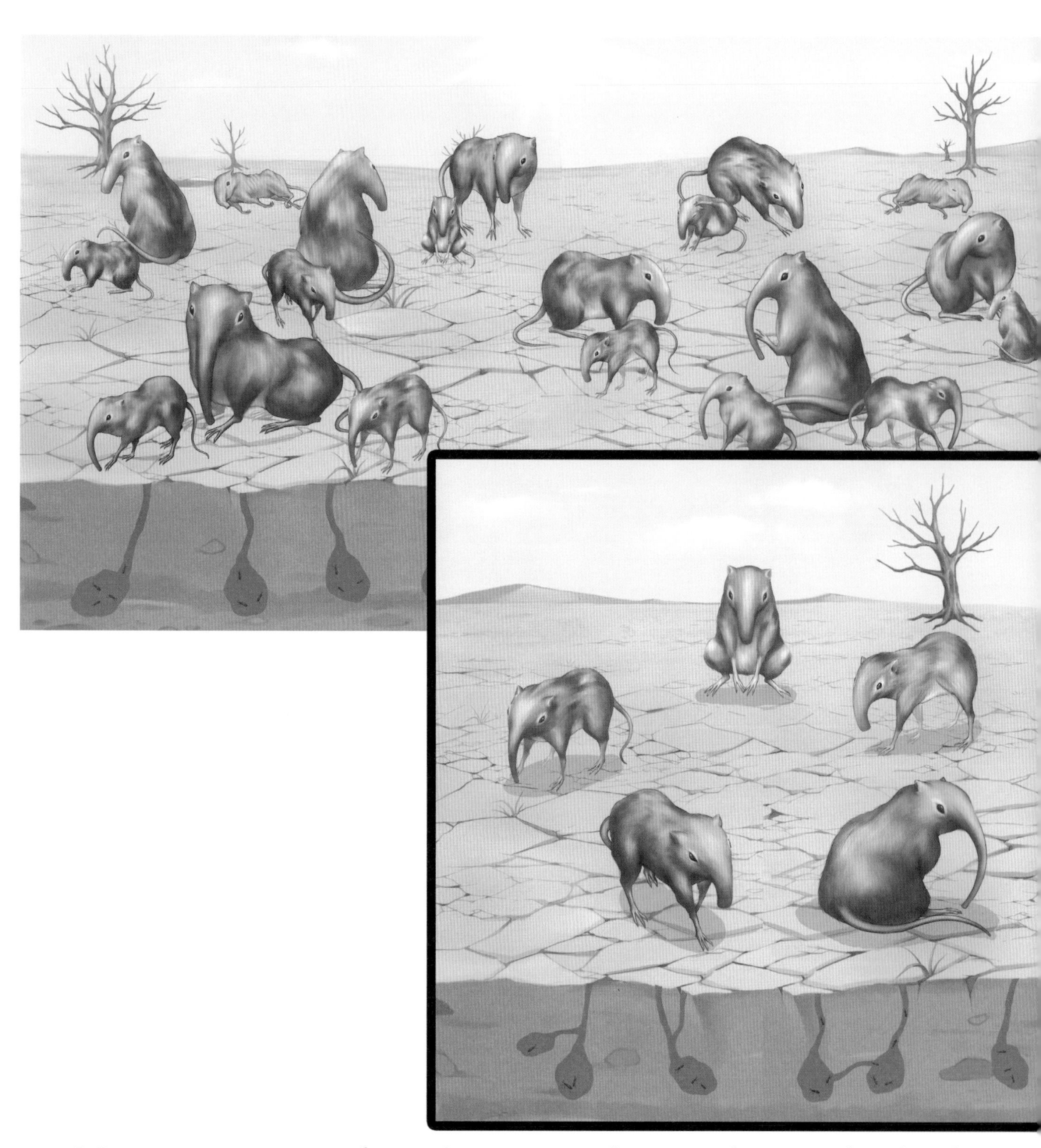

Many years went by. Time moved on. Piloses who had been healthy enough to have children after the weather became very hot, got old and died. But their children grew up to be adults. Of course, they still had the same kind of trunk they were born with because that stayed the same their whole life.

With the children fully grown and their parents gone, the group of piloses looked different than it had in the past. There were still a lot of piloses with wider trunks because there had been so many with wider trunks before the weather became very hot. But because piloses with thinner trunks had been healthier and had a lot of children each, there were more piloses with thinner trunks than before.

Time passed and the same events happened again. Piloses with thinner trunks got more milli bugs to eat, so they were healthier and each had many children born with thinner trunks just like they were. Although there were a lot of piloses with wider trunks, they were less healthy.

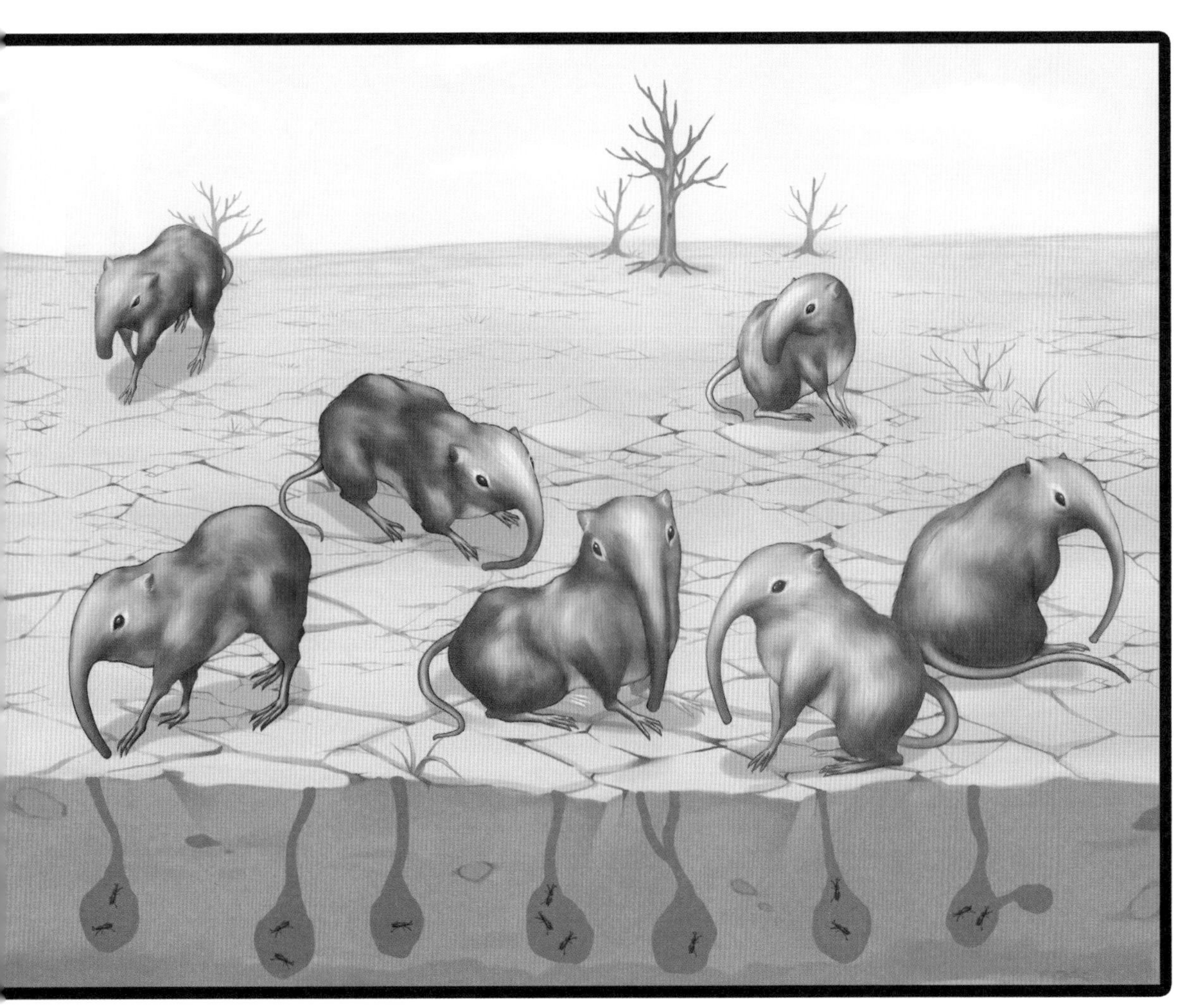

If they were able to stay alive, they only had one child born with a wider trunk just like they were. So, many years later when all these children had grown up and their parents had gotten old and died, the group looked different. So at that time, there were actually a few more piloses with thinner trunks than piloses with wider trunks.

And then this cycle happened again and again. Piloses with thinner trunks got more food so they were healthy enough to have lots of children who were born with thinner trunks like they were. These children then grew up to be adults with thinner trunks and had lots more children. Piloses with wider trunks had trouble getting food so they were less healthy and had less children.

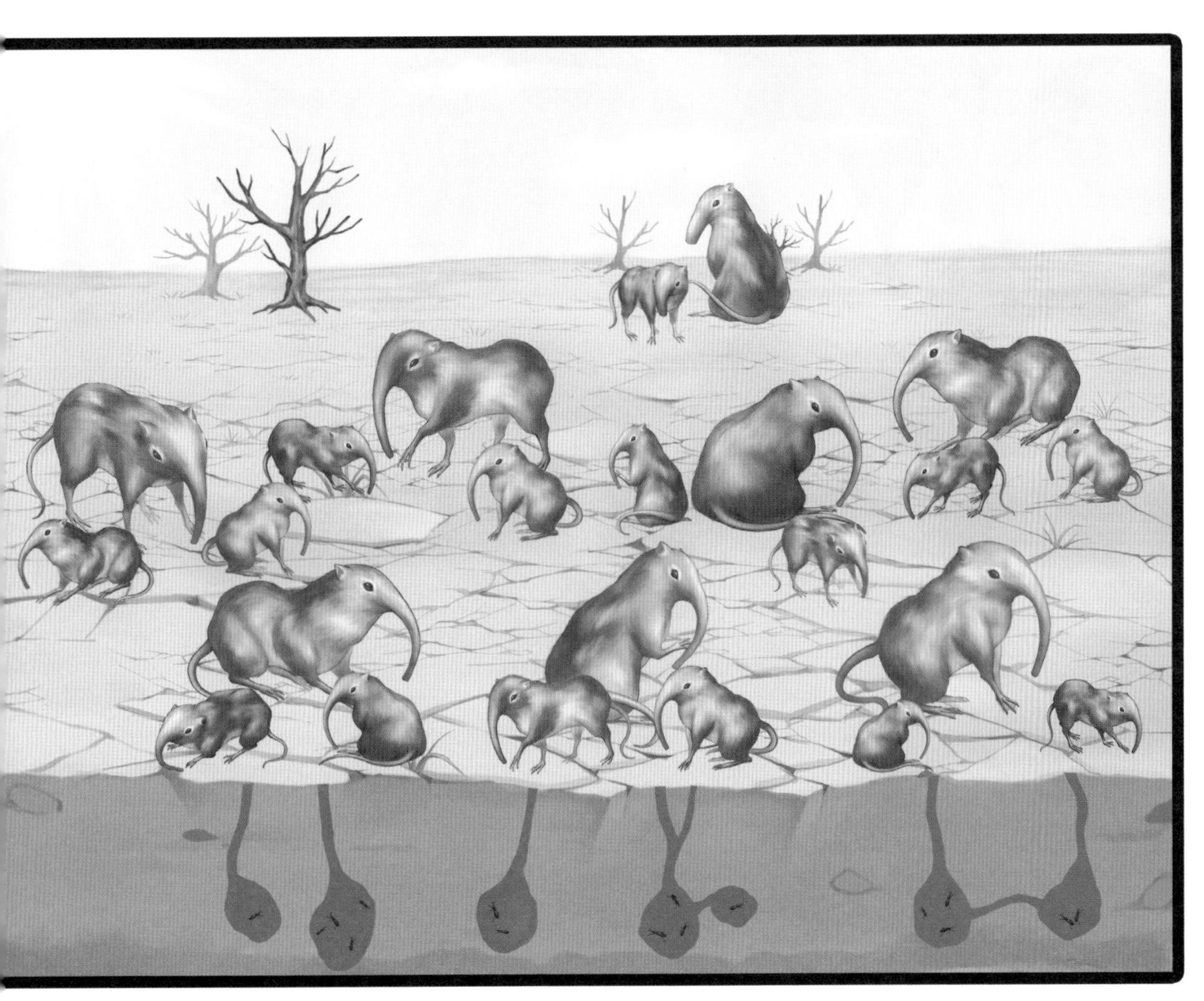

Over time and many cycles, there came to be mostly piloses with thinner trunks in the group even though there had been so many with wider trunks in the group before the weather became very hot.

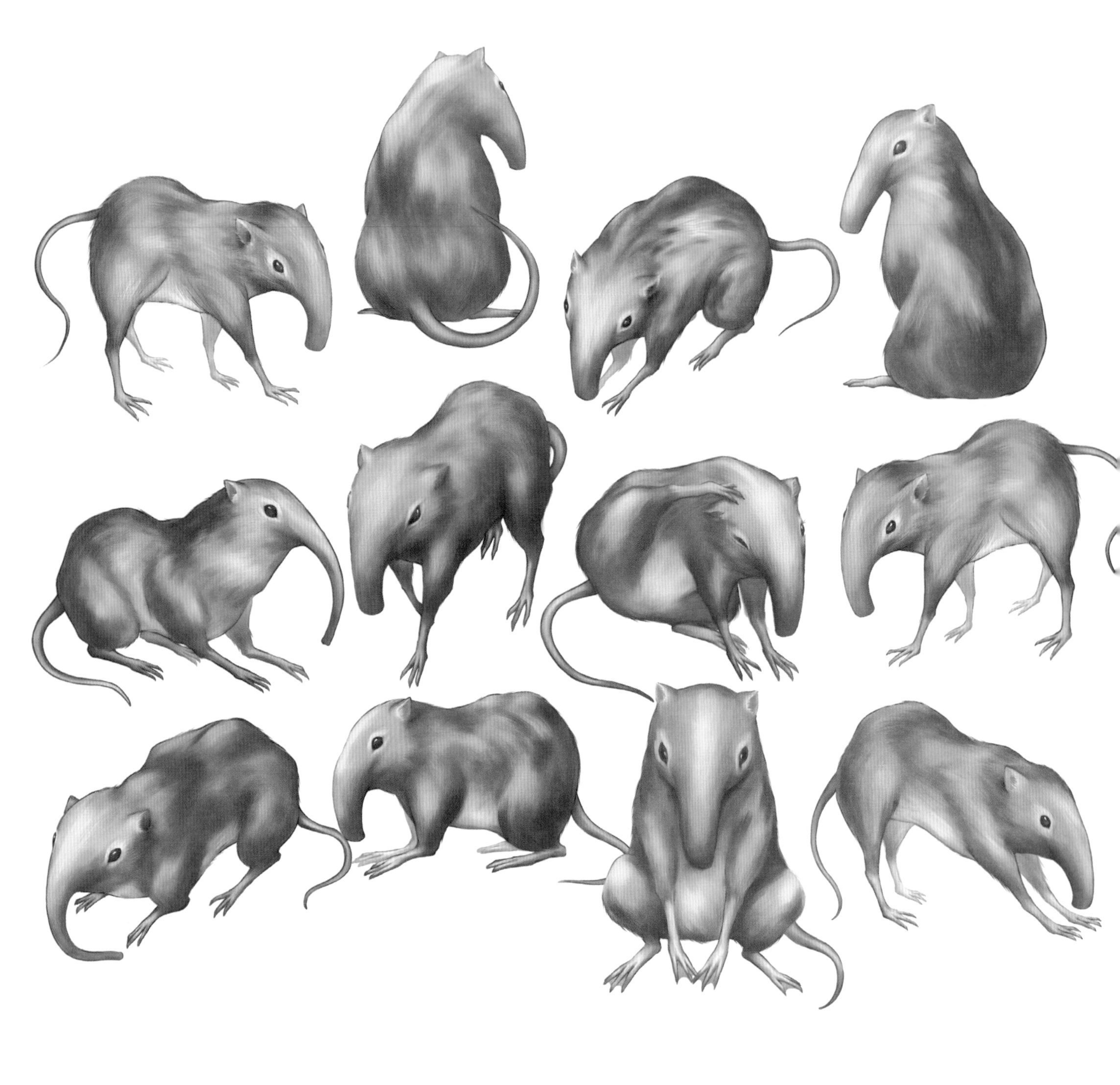

And that's how piloses went from being a group of animals with mostly wider trunks a long time ago...

to how they look nowadays. That’s why piloses mostly have thinner trunks now. That’s how piloses evolved skinny noses.

ABOUT THE AUTHOR

Deborah Kelemen, Ph.D., is a parent, child development researcher, and educator with a passion for understanding children's beliefs and feelings about the natural world. A Fellow of the Association for Psychological Sciences, she is Professor of Psychological and Brain Sciences at Boston University where she directs the Child Cognition Lab. The Lab is home to the Evolving Minds Project, a National Science Foundation-funded research group that develops educational materials to support early science learning and address common science misconceptions. Deb loves to talk about children, nature, and STEM education, and she speaks regularly in workshops, schools, and universities.

Natalie Emmons and Rebecca Seston Shillaci, former members of the Child Cognition Lab, also contributed significantly to the design, formulation, and evaluation of *How the Piloses Evolved Skinny Noses*. Other contributors to this first story in the Evolving Minds series are noted with deep gratitude in the Acknowledgments.

ACKNOWLEDGMENTS

The Child Cognition Lab team is grateful to the many contributors who made this project possible, with special thanks for the generous support of Boston University and the National Science Foundation. Our heartfelt gratitude extends as well to Dennis Hart, Jason Sweet, and the many teachers, families, and children who graciously participated in the research studies.

Project Director and Lead Researcher
Deborah Kelemen, Ph.D., Boston University

Content Development and Assessment
Natalie Emmons, Ph.D., Boston University
Rebecca Seston Schillaci, M.A., Boston University and EDC

Additional Contributors
Patricia Ganea, Ph.D.
Christopher Schneider, Ph.D.
James Traniello, Ph.D.

Evolving Minds Project Illustrations
Samantha Barry, Kristin Woo

FUNDING

This material is based in part
on work supported by
the National Science Foundation
under grants REC-0529599,
DRL-1007984,
DRL-1561401.